WHEN DINOSAURS LIVED

Tyrannosaurus rex

KATE RIGGS

Published by
CREATIVE EDUCATION

P.O. Box 227, Mankato, Minnesota 56002
Creative Education is an imprint of The Creative Company
www.thecreativecompany.us

Design and production by Danny Nanos of Gilbert & Nanos
Art direction by Rita Marshall
Printed by Corporate Graphics in the United States of America

Photographs by Alamy (Chuck Eckert, INTERFOTO),
Bridgeman Art Library (William Francis Phillipps), Corbis (Bettmann),
Getty Images (DEA Picture Library, Harry Green), iStockphoto (Jeff Chiasson,
Micha Fleuren, Klaus Nilkens, Allan Tooley), Library of Congress

Library of Congress Cataloging-in-Publication Data
Riggs, Kate.
Tyrannosaurus rex / by Kate Riggs.
p. cm.
Summary: A brief introduction to the fearsome *Tyrannosaurus rex*,
highlighting its size, habitat, food sources, and demise. Also included is a
virtual field trip to a museum with notable *T. rex* fossils.

Includes bibliographical references and index.

ISBN 978-1-60818-120-9

1. Tyrannosaurus rex—Juvenile literature. I. Title.

QE862.S3R5524 2012

567.912'9—dc22   2010049586

CPSIA: 031412 PO1557

2 4 6 8 9 7 5 3

CREATIVE EDUCATION

Table of Contents

Tyrannosaurus rex was a theropod dinosaur. It lived from 68 to 65 million years ago. The name *Tyrannosaurus rex* means "tyrant lizard king." People call it *T. rex* for short.

Each of *T. rex*'s birdlike feet had three toes with claws

T. rex was one of the scariest meat-eating dinosaurs ever! It had about 60 sharp teeth in its huge head. Its back legs were as tall as two grown-up men. But its arms were very short.

T. rex's arms were only about three feet (91 cm) long

After it hatched, *T. rex* grew quickly. An adult weighed about five tons (4.5 t). It was 40 to 50 feet (12.2–15.2 m) long, from its head to the tip of its tail. *T. rex* stood about 20 feet (6 m) tall. The towering predator chased prey at speeds as fast as 20 miles (32 km) per hour.

T. rex had a very small brain inside its huge head

T. rex lived in forests. This let it hide behind tall trees and sneak up on prey. The weather was very warm when *T. rex* was alive. Many kinds of plants covered the land.

The forests where *T. rex* lived were home to plant-eating animals

Plant-eaters such as the horned *Triceratops* and duck-billed *Edmontosaurus* lived near *T. rex*. They made good meals. The big meat-eater had to eat a lot to stay strong and active.

T. rex preyed upon many ceratopsids, or dinosaurs with horned heads

SOUND IT OUT

Edmontosaurus: *ed-MONT-oh-SORE-us* **Triceratops**: *try-SER-ah-tops*

Sometimes, *T. rex* hunted in teams. Other times, *T. rex* just waited to attack. *T. rex* died out about 65 million years ago. All the dinosaurs disappeared then.

Teams of *T. rex* could bring
down larger prey

Scientists know about *T. rex* because they have studied fossils. Fossils are the remains of living things that died long ago. Many fossils of *T. rex* have been found in the western United States. The first one was found in 1902.

Barnum Brown (bottom, left) was the first to find *T. rex* fossils

T. rex compared with a
five-foot-tall (152 cm)
person

Paleontologists are people who study dinosaurs. Henry Fairfield Osborn was the paleontologist who named *T. rex*. He called it "tyrant lizard king" because the bones were the biggest of any meat-eating dinosaur he had ever seen.

SOUND IT OUT

paleontologists: *pay-lee-ahn-TAHL-oh-jists*

People used to think that *Tyrannosaurus rex* was the biggest meat-eating dinosaur that ever lived. Now people think that another dinosaur from South America was even larger. But scientists still study *T. rex* fossils to find clues. There are more things to learn about this "tyrant lizard king"!

Older pictures of *T. rex* show its tail dragging on the ground

A Virtual Field Trip: The Field Museum, Chicago, Illinois

You can see a *Tyrannosaurus rex* named "Sue" at The Field Museum in Chicago, Illinois. It is the most complete *T. rex* skeleton on display in the world. A fossil hunter named Sue Hendrickson found the bones in 1990. Later, museum workers put all the bones together. "Sue" has been displayed since 2000, and thousands of people visit her every year.

Glossary

hatched—came out of an egg

predators—animals that kill and eat other animals

prey—animals that are killed and eaten by other animals

theropod—a meat-eating dinosaur that walked on two legs

The fossilized skull of "Sue"
weighs 600 pounds (272 kg)

Read More

Dixon, Dougal. *Meat-eating Dinosaurs*.
Mankato, Minn.: NewForest Press, 2011.

Johnson, Jinny. *Tyrannosaurus and Other Mighty Hunters*.
North Mankato, Minn.: Smart Apple Media, 2008.

Web Sites

Dinosaur Facts

http://www.thelearningpage.org/dinosaurs/dinosaur_facts.htm
This site has a fact sheet about *Tyrannosaurus rex* that can be printed out.

Enchanted Learning: Tyrannosaurus rex

http://www.enchantedlearning.com/subjects/dinosaurs/dinos/trex/index.shtml
This site has *Tyrannosaurus rex* facts and a picture to color.